POETICS

Coyote

Bainbridge Island Press

POE

Tamarah Rockwood
Editor

TICS

Coyote

Bainbridge Island Press
Bainbridge Island, WA

Volume: 2023.01 *Coyote*
POETICS is published semi-annually. Learn more and make
submissions to: https://bainbridgeisland.press/
Edited by Tamarah Rockwood

Published in 2023 by Bainbridge Island Press
Bainbridge Island, WA
https://bainbridgeisland.press

Printed in the United States of America

ISBN: 978-1-961451-03-2

Cover & Book Design: Ben Rockwood

9 8 7 6 5 4 3 2 1

Dedication

*In honor of Aristotle and his
seminal work 'Poetics' (335 BC)*

Contents

POETICS

Coyote

The Coyote that is the Apricot

By Tamarah Rockwood

To see you, the coyote
That sits on the counter on top

Of a pile of apples
So it does not bruise yet ripens

You
too quickly.

And so when I reach for you,
 You melt under my touch,

Collapsing beneath your gentle skin
So that right before I take you in my mouth

You have a hopeful thought that perhaps
You are not a coyote, but an apricot

Beginning
your own phase of metamorphosis,

Changing into something else that lives
Now

Within me.

Coyote Envy

By Collier Brown

There are worse problems
to have than this. I'll try
to explain: a child grows up
in a typical southern town,
family (good), woods and river,
lots of dead hymns and tithes,
friends, a Christmas dinner.

And yet, no sense of home
or place, no stories of
ancestral fires or the sister
rain or brother in the wild boar.
No trickster at the journey's
edge with a riddle and a lore.
Nothing on the other side.

Coyote, if you're listening,
I am not of any tribe,
I belong to no one's tale,
there is no blessing I believe,
there is no spirit I can hear.

But I've loved the dirt for all
my days, have planted flowers
ten million ways. I'd give you one,
if you'd come near.

Hey, coyote

By Elisabeth McKetta

It is a job to hoist a word
up from somewhere
and force it to grow
somewhere else.

It is a job to sun and water
a word until its roots
explode and shake.

It is a job, or is it,
to mumble into the soil,
to scale away the rot?

Somebody must spray
griffonage into ears, alleyways,
and the torn leaves of books.

Hey, poet. Hey, coyote.
You call this your life,
smuggling words
across borders.

The Call of Desire

By Tamarah Rockwood

Hush, listen closely: There are ears to hear
For calls that charm soft feet beyond these gates.
In prairie's grass, umber to umbra pelts
    Holds time as stoic, and
        waits for return.

Desire is born in the wild, when stars
Haven't dimmed, breath is hot, and dew is new.
My reply was in my breath, my high ears:
    I heard the howls when
        I was in the weeds.

It felt like calls came from our distant kin
Who lured our pups with midnight songs and sin.
But, distant they were. I answered the phone
    To say hello;
        but the ears disappeared.

The umber coyotes called since they own
The wind, the hunt, the line - from seed to stone.
Long tongues lick the wind. Their calls roam the woods
    Howling false pledges
        of bleak sisterhood.

Brazen, I called back. The seductive wild
Heard my call and the clack of my flat teeth
Over immigrant tongue, and shallow breath.
    But, I closed my lips.
        There was no reply.

Shamed by seclusion and their haughty hunt.
Laying low in the grasses is a hush.
Silence is their tender. I lack the lull
     To run with want.
         My soft feet are so bare.

I desire the bygone yearning to run.
The bright desire that lights the stars is bought
With my tender feet, and innocent heart.
     Yet, shame dulls the stars.

     I've wholly forgot.

Circle on the Prairie

By David Stallings

Outside Manhattan, Kansas, 1972

New humans are spotted
in the old limestone house,
a fast lope away
from the abandoned limestone quarry
where our pack lives.
Do they intend harm
as do so many of their kind--
trapping, poisoning, shooting us?

This afternoon one of us sees
the man walk out onto the prairie
accompanied by a dog, larger than us.
We meet, young ones yipping,
old ones barking,
and our alpha sends a dozen of us
to intercept the man and his companion.
We form a broad circle
around the two. We move as they move,
fourteen beings on the prairie.
They smell concerned, not hostile,
big dog staying close
beside the man.

For three days this continues
each afternoon, until we sense
no intended harm.

Obit for a Pickpocket

By Josh Feit
To Mary Quant, 1930-2023, with fragments from her NYT obituary

These are the aperçus of the modes of production:
--It's ridiculous, in this age of machines,
to continue to make clothes by hand. --Why can't people see
what a machine is capable of doing itself,
instead of making it copy what the hand does?

Spoken like a pickpocket of the Gods! Amateurs
at accounting emerging from post-war privation.
Her Siamese cat in the habit of eating the patterns
she purloined from Harrod's. She delighted

in pranks. Turned her nose up at anosmia. Turned
her back on the corseted shapes. Horror upon her,
she made the window displays a performance.
Upside down atelier. Spray-painted lives, mannequins
dyed or bald or clad in hurried synthetics. Couldn't stand
the guilt of one good Paris suit hanging
in the wardrobe listless like the rooms of estates.
These were the bedsit quantum mechanics of
Dame Gamine. Polyvinyl chloride prodigy.

Can we stop for a second and talk about
how beautiful Evelyn Waugh's electric guitar was?

She and this young Mr. Waugh became inseparable.
Wore mother's gold silk pajamas to class,
ran their fears and wash & wears
like a coffee bar. She cried on her
13th birthday because she knew horror was getting
closer.

--The young should look like the young.
--The most extreme fashion should be very cheap.

Passers-by sneered: "God, look at this Modern Youth!"

Shall we be Modern Youth tonight?
These are the aperçus in obituaries.

--First, because only the young are daring enough to wear it;
second, because the young look better in it;
and third, because it shall not last.

Courage v. Comfort

By Rayne Lacko

A coyote

      (Canis latrans, singing dog)

Tests the air.

The scent of dinner

      (Felis catus, indoor cat allowed outdoors)

clings to nearby salal

      (tucked for slumber under a blanket of fog and moonlight).

A trail is detected

      (tiny imprints in moist soil).

Wheaten hairs bristle about coyote's plush neck

      (a Medal of Honor for frequent successes in battle).

Cunning, agile muscles lunge to snatch

      (the cat from where it hides)

Lone coyote shares nothing, feeding only

the thick, rusted-red regal cloak

      (gleaming in the emerald woods).

Of a cedar crowned island.

Coyote bays her pack's song

      (Linked by the rhythm).

Lone coyote returns to the pack's warm den.

The wild calls the wild: the fighter, the audacious

      (Audax omnia perpeti, ready to dare all).

Unafraid to share the night, be seen. Presence known,

      (Yet not devoured).

Cat's full dish, and bed by warm fire, await her return.

Never
By Gary Wood

Coyote wakes me up
in the middle of the busy dream
to which I have consigned myself,
pokes fun at my encapsulating plans and assumptions
howls with delight to frustrate my expectations
stumbles me if necessary, with a stone in my path
teaches me, again, the lesson of my petty distractions
reminds me of the journey thus far, the journey ahead
the cosmic humor of existence
the companionship that I am never truly alone...

Coyote Season

By Elisabeth McKetta

In the dark-night pregnant winter, three cold weeks before my daughter was born, my husband and I went for a drive. Our lives were about to change and we were trying not to talk about it. We live where city meets wild in tamed unexpected corners--in baseball outfields or behind hospitals, where lives come and go. And so this night we saw a coyote.

She was playing with her pups in a ditch that ran along the road. She had something in her mouth that she tossed in the air, and then waited for her babies to catch: a beautiful nonsense game of her own. Just a mother, playing. A headlight flickered, and in its light, we saw feathers; we knew then that the thing was a bird.

Soon another coyote arrived--the father? we wondered. He saw where the bird had been. He guarded it from her, from them. She pounced off and her pups followed. She did not care what happened to the bird. It was only feathers, after all. The male lost interest, saw us in the car waiting with the lights off, and hid. The mother re-found the bird, tossed it and caught it again. She was slender, quick, all tail and play. She buried her toy under leaves, then vanished. It was the only secretive thing we saw her do all night.

I thought she was the most beautiful mother I had ever seen. A coyote can be anything she wants. I was cartoonishly pregnant, big-belly-heavy with that low-headed baby. Nowhere in my body could I find energy to play like that.

All night my confused dreams chased their tails and flung dead birds up and down the ladder of my spine. I knew that when the baby came I would find a way. I would huddle with my babies behind the trees, would be all tail and play, would toss precious things in the air, not caring if I have eaten, not caring if I am seen, or who is nearby. I would play with my babies, flinging life at them without showing them my fear that we lived each day at the edge of life and death. I would remember her, and learn to be a good mammal, after all.

Summer Day on Bainbridge Island

By Mary Lou Sanelli

I am not the least bit drawn to the center
of town, where tourists pack the sidewalks
and the shopping is like anywhere in the world
where people have money to spend.
Instead, I bike to Manzanita Bay
to sit cross-legged on the sand
under a rare, warm sun and see nothing
but this green and peopled land
where nearly every view leaves me
sighing in appreciation.
(Even if that sounds schmaltzy, or whatever,
I don't care. It's true.)
And to join my friend Pam
who I don't know well, but meeting at the beach
is a good start, isn't it?
A man walks by, reeking of coconut oil and beer,
his stench yeasty. When he stops to slice an orange
in two, juice dripping down his fingers,
I think Oh! A man with a knife
instead of an iPhone?
How manly is that?
Pam swims but I can't get in.
I wished then, as I wish now,
that I could be better at taking a plunge.
I don't remember every other detail
about our sun drenched afternoon
but I do remember how the wind came up
and blew the lid off a beachgoer's cooler
and how, for a moment, the sand was sharp as glass against my cheek.
I remember thinking how Pam looked happy in the water, relaxed,
and how this seemed perfectly natural
and fitting because, of course, the sea heals.
I remember the man running up to a car to open the door
for a woman in a short green dress.
I remember his strong, hairy forearm held her close.
I remember he reached for the small of her back

and gave it a little squeeze--huge
gesture to her, though. (And me!)
I remember sensing, he loves her.

What I'm getting at is this: It's easy to believe in love
on a summer day on a scenic island.
Easier still to trust that when we fall in love,
someone will catch us.
I like to believe in men
capable of such a catch.
I stared at the two of them.
I pretended not to. But once I started,
I couldn't stop.
I had this thought
that things between them would turn out "just fine."
If "just fine" is a man who will not only open a car door
but his ... I am looking for a better, less obvious, word here ...
but there is none, so I will say it: heart.
And then, there it was!
The most unforgettable image of the day
running forward and sort of sideways at once.
You know what I mean, right?
That funny gait coyotes have.
"I hate to go," Pam said,
"but I have to round up my chickens!"
Later that evening, I heard a cayote howling
near my place by the ferry landing.
A coincidence? Or a memory
of what nights were like before electricity
lit dark days and darker nights and technology
turned everything into another kind of "experience."
A perfect reminder that nature still offers
the most remarkable things.

Coy O te

By Kristi Helgeson

All those hours in front of the TV and Wile E. Coyote
never caught the Roadrunner. Each time he dropped

an anvil off a desert plateau or opened an ACME crate
of dynamite we cheered for him to no avail. But here

in our suburban enclave he takes no prisoners only
carcasses -- wild rabbits, the neighbor's indoor cat who

got out, and a chihuahua named Pee Wee Herman
who went out without his coyote vest for

the last time. After these feral murders we interrogated
the name of the accused because we are people who

play with words and so we broke it into parts
like jaws crunching into bones and we thought

long and hard about these things like how coyotes
really are coy, shrinking from contact with us, but we

remove trees, level lots, pour foundations so now it's so
hard to hide, and how strange it is, no, it's funny, really, that

O te is the Japanese command for Shake!

Happy Sabbath

By Veron Graham

he is walking quickly
his time for hunger growing tall
small towns can only hold him
'til he finds another place to fall

he will stop soon to breathe
please hold him inside your mind
another quest's already forming
but he's running out of time

he wears a feather on his back
you can hear it whistle in the flight
"como corres?" It's always asking
'til he howls into the night

Boston Sightings

By Collier Brown

First, you have to know that cats
don't even stray from door flaps
and wet food, not in Boston, where
a hawk sometimes crashes into glass
or a pigeon, scuffed by baffled
pedestrians, recognizes his
own kind stalking senseless too,
along the streets, then instantly forgets.

Unworried by predation, they've lost
a vigilance behind the skull,
imagination gone inert, unexercised.
The city's unanimaled estate,
the vacant nests of the carbon fog.
That's not to say the wild dog
doesn't live here too, even the coyote.

It's rumored a few still rove. In the news,
someone's outdoor pet got nabbed,
someone's food delivery mauled
and chewed. Then a spotting by the church
or in the schoolyard, near the swings.

Here's a story: cemetery
down the block from me,
acres of fenced-in trees, hiding ground
with hedges and high grass. I was out
walking, just passing through,
and that extra sight we call
"the corner" of the eye, it noticed
a thing it had learned to see
without seeing, thousands of years
ago. The coyote's glare, the dart
of it, its theft of pulse, thin chill.

Do you measure between
yourself and harm by feet, by sweat,
by time? I could have thrown a stone,
that's what I mean. Or no, what I mean
is that she knew that I was there.

And not that it matters, not that it
changes a thing, but the sound of heavy
machinery nearby (July roadwork,
the crack and hammer, crush, clack,
and grind) made me dizzy, blank,
and without--how to do I say it?--a world.

That was some time ago. I haven't
seen her since. I haven't thought
to say again, She knew that I was there.
The hawks still crash into the glass,
pigeons stagger in the tar.
My street goes ten new ways away.
She's not the one who'd go that far.

The Hunter

By Leah Haight

I didn't know I was running
from you until
you appeared and blocked
my path, hounding me
until I said your name

Coyote

I was like you, once,
a roamer
who feasted on opportunity,
a wanderer
primed to relish good fortune

but I killed you.

I hunted you
and shot you,
stripped you of the
only thing worth keeping: your pelt
an artifact of my conquest.

So don't show up now,
Yote,
baiting me back
to the wild with you.
I don't want that life,
go, leave me alone.

I don't belong
under the open sky like you do,
a scavenger
enduring weeks without food,
a survivor
dodging bullets while
yipping your triumph
that the hunted
is now the hunter.

Enough of this.
I concede I cannot be rid of you.
Take a piece of my flesh,
skin for skin,
and grant me your absolution.

Alone I Travel

By Gary Wood

Alone, I travel unaware
as he scurries his trickster's trail not far behind
follows my silent scent, without relent as I be blind
weaving left, weaving right, just out of sight
his private cunning, darting, running,
I am as his clumsy prey, his delight
This night, emboldened, my shelter nears,
without fears, the path seems clear
but twists up and circles down around
then stumbles into the thorny thicket of my fragiled life
My relentless coyote, then yips and screams and squalls,
my blood aflush with fears, I turn, I fall,
into the darkest brambled night
his pack joins in, the howls, the shrieks from all around
laughing at my hapless helpless plight
I am the awkward creature here,
unprepared, humbled, scared
The message sent, the jokesters' fall silent into the dark
and disappear into the night

Coyote Story

By John McKetta

California is a land steeped in myth. Beyond the well-worn cli-chés about Hollywood, the Gold Rush, and the myth of the unattain-able American Dream, the land itself — its hilltops, crests, and cracked riverbeds — is part of a wider tapestry of Native storytelling stretching for thousands of miles both north and east, creating a vast "L" connect-ing Southern Canada to Central Texas, weaving its way across what is now the Southwestern United States. Within this tapestry, stories ebb and flow; plots remain consistent, but the animals trade their roles to suit each storyteller's geography. As you travel north, Hawk becomes Eagle, Turtle is replaced by Beaver. Yet throughout all of these tales, one character remains a constant, dancing his way through the mythos of each land — Navajo, Tongva, Pueblo, Crow — always elusive, always incandescent. This, of course, is Coyote.

I grew up immersed in Coyote stories, translated into my own language and recorded on a series of off-white cassette tapes that my sisters and I would obsessively rewind and fast forward, rewind and fast-forward, reliving our favorite stories as we basked in the calm, lan-guid voice of Joe Hayes — the Fred Rogers of the American Southwest. I listened in rapt fascination as Coyote shimmied his way across the tales, recalibrating his moral compass to suit the needs of each story. In one story, he creates humans, molding us in his own image while the other animals are asleep. Later, he gives us fire. Then, in the very next story, he condemns our species to death, tricking us out of our chance at immortality. In one story, he is Prometheus, in the next Loki, here Lucifer, there Christ. To this day, I can think of no other god who is quite so human. But even then, as a child in Texas, I knew that real coyotes — the ones with the lower-case "c" — weren't like that. They were dangerous, loathsome, terrifying beasts.

* * *

I moved to Los Angeles shortly after college. I managed to find a house in the hills overlooking the Arroyo Seco canyon which the real-tor described as "a little oasis in the city." It was idyllic. Most mornings I woke up to birdsong.

But soon the howling began. During the day, they were nowhere to be found — you couldn't even find traces of them. But at night you could hear them feasting. Shortly after moving in with me, my partner lost both of her cats — first Alice and then Jasper — to the coyotes. Coyotes prefer to hunt under the light of a full moon, and we would track the lunar phases each month with a growing sense of dread. On moonlit nights, my partner and I would sit in our living room, listening to the screams of our neighbor's pets dying on the other side of the mountain. The howls echoed throughout the canyon, rattling their way into our homes, lurching across our kitchen tables, before finally digging their way into our chests. Every full moon, for a few short minutes, it became impossible to believe that we were truly safe, fully removed from it all. Carnage was always close at hand. The next morning, retrieving our morning newspapers, we would glance sheepishly at our neighbors, doing our best to smile through the aftershocks of shared fear: *"Did you hear the howling last night? Someone was hungry!" "I know, right? It woke us up!" "Us too! Haw haw!"* And then silence. A bird chirped, one of us might have coughed. If we had worn watches, we would have checked them. *"Anyway, stay safe." "You too."* A friendly wave and then back to the air-conditioned hum of our houses, making sure the door clicked behind you as you crossed the threshold, giving the dog an extra treat with her breakfast but not quite understanding why.

Eventually, some of the neighbors began to fight back. They had moved to the neighborhood to be closer to nature, and, whatever "nature" was, the coyotes had stolen it from them. Arguments broke out on online message boards over the ethics of baiting them with rat poison. Up the hill from us, one family bought a rifle. Sometimes, when I walked my dog early in the morning, we passed a lone coyote in the street, heading home late after a night of unsuccessful hunting. If a car drove by, the driver would often swerve, trying to hit it. Unsuccessful, they would then honk until it ran off into the woods.

Around this time, my partner and I decided to get a second dog. She had just started a new job and I had just lost one; we suspected we might not have this particular balance of disposable income and abundant free time in our lives again anytime soon. Besides, we had always wanted a border collie.

We found a litter in the Antelope Valley, a region of lush, poppy-laden hills about an hour and a half north of us. We fell in love with a red merle — a rare pattern for border collies consisting of Van Gogh-ish splashes of brown, tan, and chestnut — and filled out the adoption forms that day. We called our puppy Oola, a name she chose herself, but that is another story altogether. It's a funny thing: everyone always thinks their puppy is the cutest animal alive. It just so happened that ours actually was.

But when we brought Oola home, our neighbors weren't quite as keen on her. As we arrived home, cradling our squirming bushel of fur, one neighbor skittled cooingly up to our driveway. But as they drew nearer, their pace slowed, their expression transforming into one of confusion, bordering on disgust. Soon, the moment passed and social instincts kicked back in: *"Oh my gawd! Would you look at her. Him? Her? And that, that color… you know, you don't really see that color in a dog that often, do you? So unusual!"*

At the dog park, Oola was afraid of other dogs. Absolutely petrified. Shepherds and huskies and even other collies would come bounding over, nudging her to play with them, and she would curl up into a ball, tail tucked, huffing like a hedgehog until they left. There was no sense of a connection, no intraspecies bond. It was as though she was unable to recognize anything of herself in other dogs. We consulted dog-parenting books, we called our vet. The advice was always the same: just keep socializing her, just keep trying.

In the following months, Oola adapted to our schedules and the pace of our lives. She learned to play fetch, to ask to be let out, to sit, stay, pretend to enjoy kibble, all of the tricks we demand of our domesticated companions. But whenever there was a full moon, that all changed. We'd sit huddled in our living room, cringing with each howl, my partner and I breathing deeply, trying to remain calm while our older dog barked and gritted her teeth. But Oola was enraptured. She would run the length of the house, peering out the windows, whimpering to be let out. Whatever was making that noise, Oola was desperate to see it.

When she was nine months old, she got her chance. We were stepping out the door for our morning walk, when our older dog began to growl. Standing in the lawn directly across the street from us was a fully grown male coyote. We froze. From fifteen feet away, we could smell the dust and iron emanating from his fur. Ignoring us, the coyote craned his neck, staring intently at something just beyond our knees. Behind us, little Oola stood transfixed. In a single motion, she jerked free of her collar and crossed the street. She and the coyote stood nose to nose, eyeing one another. In that moment, it struck me that, though their proportions were completely different, the patterns and colors of their coats were nearly identical. Oola looked like a misshapen coyote pup. And after months of anxious dog park visits, she was calmer than we'd ever seen her.

The coyote turned to leave and Oola turned with him. We lunged forward, trying to catch her, but we were too late. In an instant, they were off, Oola and her coyote, sprinting up the hill towards the meadows. We screamed, yelled, ran until our lungs burned. Neighbors spilled out of their houses and joined in the chase. It was no use, though. They were far too fast for our human legs. After twenty minutes of searching, we returned home to get the car. There, panting on the doorstep, sat Oola, smiling from ear to doggy ear. For the first time in her life, she had met another creature that looked like her, that recognized her. She had found a friend. And she was ecstatic.

I'd like for this story to end here. It's where I wish I could end it. Because I think that would be really nice: a story about two species, one hated, the other adored, finding common ground and affection. But that isn't how it ends.

The next time Oola saw coyotes from our balcony, she was excited and we were too. But as the months passed, she began socializing with other dogs. She learned to run with a pack at the dog park, to sniff and be sniffed, to wag beckoningly at our neighbors when they passed her in the street. On clear nights, when she heard the howls echoing across the neighborhood, Oola began to join our older dog in barking at them. One day, she saw another coyote on the street and she growled at him. Oola had chosen her side — something was telling her that she now belonged to a world of humans and house pets and that coyotes were not welcome in that reality. The bond was broken.

She was somebody's dog now.

* * *

I've often wondered why it is that humans never tried to domesticate coyotes. Seeing Oola standing next to one, it became difficult to rationalize why one of these creatures was a pet and the other was a pest. But when you look into a coyote's eyes, you see something you don't often see when looking at a house pet: there is a fierce and steady independence, unimpressed and seemingly disinterested in humans. It is an utterly disarming experience.

We've trained much of our world to need us. We've domesticated our companion animals to blunt their sharp edges; we've uprooted the forests, diverted the streams, and paved over the marshes. The nature we encounter in our cities tends to require some level of *upkeep*, it needs our support, or at least we are able to believe that it does. The alternative is perhaps too painful to imagine: not being needed. How awful it is to think that all of these changes we've inflicted on our planet might be unnecessary, or, even worse, insignificant. So, when we look into a coyote's eyes and we encounter that intelligence, that unimpressed independence — the very traits we value in humans — it shakes us. Because as long as it is watching us, some part of us knows that we aren't in control, not really, not like we wish we were. So, we honk our horns, we pick up our rocks and throw them, anything to get the coyote to leave us alone, hoping it will stay away forever this time. But I don't think we could bear that type of loneliness. I think some part of us needs to be seen as the coyote sees us.

In the old stories, humans seek out Coyote when we are in trouble. When times are easier — when we have warmth and food and the Moon and his brothers aren't trying to kill us — we invariably go back to distrusting him, avoiding him, banishing him from our villages. But when the world is on fire or it becomes too dry for life, we open our doors again and howl, begging him to come back and save us.

References

Dove, M., Guie, H. and McWhorter, L., 2013. *Coyote Stories*. Lincoln: UNP - Bison Books.
Hayes, J. and Castro López, A., 2011. *The Coyote Under the Table*. El Paso, TX: Cinco Puntos Press.
Hayes, J. and Jelinek, L., 1983. *Coyote &: Native American Folk Tales*. Santa Fe, N.M.: Mariposa Pub.
Judson, K., 1994. *Myths and Legends of California and the Old Southwest*. Lincoln, Neb.: University of Nebraska Press